A Walk through the
LOWLAND RAIN FOREST
of Sabah

Elaine J.F. Campbell

with photographs by
C.L. Chan, A.Y.C. Chung, M. Heydon, A. Lamb, F. Lanting,
B.S. Parris, W.M. Poon, M. Strange, R. Stuebing, and K.M. Wong

line illustrations by
Jamal Hassim

edited by
K.M. Wong

Natural History Publications (Borneo) Sdn. Bhd.
Kota Kinabalu

in association with

Borneo Rainforest Lodge
Danum Valley, Lahad Datu,
Sabah, Malaysia

1994

Natural History Publications (Borneo) Sdn. Bhd.,
A928, 9th Floor, Wisma Merdeka,
P.O. Box 13908,
88846 Kota Kinabalu, Sabah, Malaysia

in association with

Borneo Rainforest Lodge,
Innoprise Corporation Sdn. Bhd.,
P.O. Box 11623,
88817 Kota Kinabalu,
Sabah, Malaysia.

First published 1994

A Walk through the *LOWLAND RAIN FOREST* of Sabah

ISBN 983-812-002-2 (Limpback)
ISBN 983-812-004-9 (Hardcover)

Printed and bound in Malaysia
by Print & Co. Sdn. Bhd., Kuala Lumpur.

CONTENTS

FOREWORD

Photo: C.L. Chan

Every now and then, we are confronted with the necessity of evaluating successes and failures in conservation. Conservation without education would be blind, and requires to be supported by the information which research brings forth. The Sabah Foundation, its development and scientific research and training programmes, especially at the Danum Valley Field Studies Centre, and its continuing emphasis on supporting publications that contribute towards knowledge and awareness about conservation and natural history, contribute towards this philosophy. Our support for this book is wholeheartedly forthright, as it addresses an important aspect: the tropical lowland rain forest in Sabah and Borneo.

Special mention might be made of the Danum Valley Conservation Area, which is the largest expanse of protected lowland rain forest in Sabah, and one of the few truly excellent centres for tropical rainforest research in the world. It is already well known to even the foremost of scientists and conservationists and, I am proud to say, school children as well, for they are the human resource of the future. Internationally recognised for its facilities for research into rainforest functioning, which lay the foundation for sustainable forest management, it is also an exciting area for wilderness recreation, especially with the development of the Borneo Rainforest Lodge as an exclusive facility for natural history tourism. Elaine Campbell is one of the few scientists who have known the Danum Valley from its inception as a conservation area, and who have continued to carry out her studies on the rain forest there. The Danum Valley continues to play a pivotal role in our efforts at conservation and education, and this book by Elaine Campbell translates the wonders of the rain forest for the general reader. The facts of the rain forest and its special characteristics ought to be well known to even more people. This book, and others which describe our forests and its natural history, are the important building blocks in the fostering of a general wisdom, if not conscience, about our natural environment.

I feel a special sense of pride that Elaine has responded to this need for an account of the rain forest such as this. Inspired by the conservation opportunities such as those represented by the Danum Valley effort, and by scientific workers who keep in mind public education and awareness even as they continue their complex studies of the great rain forest, I am confident that the example provided by this book shall bring forth more interest in producing books that are accessible to all. To keep nature alive, we must bring nature to live, in as many ways as possible. This book is one of those vital pathways, and I am privileged to introduce it.

Tengku D.Z. Adlin
President,
The Sabah Society,
Kota Kinabalu
May 1994

vii

Lowland rain forest, at dawn. (*Photo: Frans Lanting/Minden Pictures*)

RAIN FOREST

The romance and imagery of the tropical rain forest has intrigued humans since the first European explorers visited and wrote about the "Indies" in the late 1500's. The jungle invoked visions of impenetrable vegetation, drenched with rain, overflowing with unfamiliar and perhaps dangerous animals. It was overpowering and apparently untamable, a strange yet mysterious place, irresistible and seductive. Even today, for the uninitiated and veteran visitor alike, a trip into rain forest still provides a sense of questing after knowledge, exploring the unknown, with the possibility of a little adventure along the way.

The term Tropical Lowland Rain Forest is used to describe the forest found in perpetually wet tropical areas where there is little or no seasonal water shortage and the climate is continuously warm and humid. In the lowland rain forest of Borneo temperatures average around 31°C during the day and 22.5°C at night. The humidity at its lowest is around 70% in the middle of the day but reaches 100% at night.

Borneo is the third largest island in the world and lowland rain forest vegetation which occurs from sea level to about 750 m or sometimes even 1200 m, covers most of the island. Above these altitudes another forest formation called montane forest occurs. Within lowland rain forest the vegetation varies depending on the type of rock substrate and soils which underly it, together with its proximity to salt water.

Most of Sabah's remaining pristine lowland rain forest is found in the eastern half of the state. The largest rain forest areas occurs between the two largest rivers, the Segama and Kinabatangan, and north to Sandakan Bay. The great diversity of plants in the Bornean lowland rain forests makes it a botanical paradise; the forest contains at least two thousand types of tree as well as an amazing variety of herbs, shrubs and other plant forms.

This great variety of plants has come about partly because since the geological past much of the region of present-day Borneo was an archipelago of islands which was enriched by species that had spread from the adjacent northern and southern ancient land masses. The isolation of plants and animals on these islands during the Tertiary Period, 15-70 million years ago, also fostered the evolution of many new species. The continuous warm, moist conditions in these forests, due to their proximity to the equator and the plentiful rainfall, have allowed many plants and animals to co-exist and evolve together on soils which are generally very poor in nutrients.

The Staghorn Fern, *Platycerium coronarium*, another epiphytic fern. The reservoir of nutrients collected by the leaf bases of this fern is also sometimes exploited by other plants, such as orchids. *(Photo: B.S. Parris)*

COMMON FEATURES OF SABAH'S LOWLAND RAIN FOREST

On entering the forest you may be overwhelmed by its stately nature, as if entering a dark, emerald cathedral with lofty trees forming tall pillars around you. Among these immense trees are smaller ones, creating a green and brown patchwork of leaves and bark.

Sunlight filtering down through chinks in the canopy casts bright, but short-lived, flecks of light on the dark, wet forest floor. The lower light intensity and different spectral quality at the lowest levels of the forest imposes constraints on plant growth, and the adaptations to survive in this environment includes the development of striking red, silvery, or iridescent green or blue colourations in the leaves. All these variations in colouration are adaptations to increase the absorption and refraction of light onto the light-trapping pigments in the leaf tissues.

With their distinctive crowns and trunks which often rise to heights over 40 m, dipterocarp trees give the Bornean rain forest its majestic appearance. Dipterocarp trees, from their family name Dipterocarpaceae,

Surviving coils of a liana fallen with its supporting tree, which has since died and rotted away. *(Photo: E.J.F. Campbell)*

Dipterocarp trees are common, such as this emergent, belonging to the timber group known as "selangan batu". *(Photo A. Lamb)*

The two-winged fruits of a "keruing" tree, *Dipterocarpus borneensis.*
(Photo: K.M. Wong)

are found in greater abundance in Bornean lowland rain forest than anywhere else in South East Asia. They thus give the lowland rain forest its more commonly known name, lowland dipterocarp forest. The word "di-ptero-carp" means "two-winged-fruit" and comes from the wing-like appendages of the mature fruits, although not all species in the family have two wings in their fruit. Five-winged fruits and fruits with no wings also occur. Strong winds can blow the ripe fruits from dipterocarp tree branches and the spinning wings, acting like helicopter blades, help to ensure that the fruits are dispersed away from the mother tree.

Dipterocarp trees form the main source for Sabah's hardwood timber, much of which is highly prized for its strength and beauty. Two lesser-known forest products are also collected from dipterocarp trees. The first is illipe oil which is squeezed out of the nut of some species and used in making chocolate. The second is "damar", a resin produced by dipterocarp trees in response to bark damage. The "damar" solidifies in contact with air and helps trees resist attack and infection by fungi, bacteria and insects. "Damar" is collected and exported for use in the paint, varnish and linoleum industries.

One of the very many species of *Cyrtandra*, a diverse genus in the family of the African Violets (Gesneriaceae). *(Photo: C.L. Chan)*

Stilt roots, though characteristic, sometimes give an impression of tree trunks supported above the forest floor. *(Photo: E.J.F. Campbell)*

Fruits of the forest durian, *Durio testudinarum*, produced near the base of the trunk, an example of cauliflory. *(Photo: A. Lamb)*

Large rain forest trees often have huge buttress roots at the base of their trunks. Most lowland forest soils are shallow, preventing trees from producing a deep taproot. Tree roots thus grow outwards away from the base of the trunk instead of down. Although the biomechanics of buttress roots is little studied, it appears that buttresses may help to support the tree and reduce susceptibility to being uprooted. Smaller rain forest trees sometimes have aerial or stilt-like roots that develop from the lower portion of the trunk and which grow into the soil and thicken. These stilt roots act in a similar manner to buttress roots and are more common in species which grow in areas prone to flooding, such as along river banks and in swampy forests.

The bark of rain forest trees richly varies in colour and texture, ranging from black to white, through fawn to bright orange and reddish-brown. Some trees have smooth bark whereas others have intricate patterns of fissures and ridges, peeling, cracking and flaking bark. Both bark and root characters are often used by foresters to help them identify certain types of tree.

Many trees which occur in the forest understorey bear their flowers and fruits on their trunks, a phenomenon called cauliflory. Brightly coloured flowers and fruits produced low down on the trunk of these smaller trees attract many birds, small mammals and insects to act as pollinators and seed dispersers. It may be that the stillness of the air in the dense understorey restricts small trees using wind to pollinate their flowers, as their branches never reach the forest canopy where winds are present.

On the other hand, two other characteristic life forms, the epiphytes and lianas, have many species with wind dispersed fruits, seeds or spores produced high up in the forest canopy. Epiphytes are plants which grow on the surface of others, commonly spending their entire life in a tree's crown or on the trunk. Many diverse plant types have epiphytic members including ferns, lichens, mosses, orchids and other flowering plants. Lianas, or woody climbers, on the other hand, often start life on the forest floor using trees and each other to climb into the forest canopy to reproduce. Many of the smaller understorey trees can be burdened with many liana stems.

After taking only a few steps inside the forest, you will begin to perspire due to the high humidity. Fortunately, there are so many other sensations to experience that you will quickly cease to notice being uncomfortable. The rich and earthy aroma from the profusion of living and decaying plant material, with the occasional hint of fragrance from forest flowers, will hopefully draw you further into the forest.

Cauliflory, the habit of bearing flowers on the trunk, in a tree of the Annonaceae (Soursop) family. *(Photo: E.J.F. Campbell)*

Buttressed tree trunks, common in lowland tropical rain forest. *(Photo: C.L. Chan)*

Active from the first hours of morning, the Bornean Gibbon (*Hylobates muelleri*) forms small family groups to defend a territory of some 20-30 ha. *(Photo: M. Strange)*

AROUND DAWN

Often the most exciting part of the day is around dawn when the ghostly mist shrouding the forest canopy slowly lifts, evaporating in the warmth of the sun. The silence is broken by the rich whooping and gurgling calls of Bornean Gibbons (*Hylobates muelleri*) in the tree tops, proclaiming their territories.

Although gibbons are less likely to flee while calling, one should still approach a group quietly. All of Sabah's primates have very keen eyesight and often detect human presence long before you have a chance to glimpse them. Admire the grace and agility of the gibbons swinging away through the trees after spotting you. Usually these animals do not move very far, but hide among the foliage of another tree and watch you curiously as you try again to locate them. All arboreal primates flee through the canopy to safety when disturbed. The Pig-tailed Macaque (*Macaca nemestrina*), on the other hand, is more terrestrial and if disturbed will often jump to the ground to escape, crashing down through the undergrowth and running off.

As the sun filters down to the forest floor, a dawn chorus of bird song can be heard from the forest. The harsh caws of Slender-billed Crows (*Corvus enca*) are mixed in with the varied calls of numerous other birds, ranging from the cheerful but tuneless Straw-headed Bulbul (*Pycnonotus zeylanicus*), to the complex and melodious calls of the White-rumped Shama (*Copyschus malabaricus*), which rivals that of the nightingale.

The Pig-tailed Macaque (*Macaca nemestrina*) moves around in groups of up to 30 individuals, often quite noisily. (*Photo: C.L. Chan.*)

11

Some other bird calls which will definitely attract your attention are the raucous cackles and noisy wing flapping of hornbills in the forest canopy high above you. All eight Bornean species occur in eastern Sabah. Each species has a distinctive call. The Rhinoceros Hornbill (*Buceros rhinoceros*) has a characteristic roaring call, the Helmeted Hornbill (*Rhinoplax vigil*) gives a long series of hoots which gradually speed up and climax in a mocking laugh, while the Bushy-crested Hornbill *(Anorrhinus galeritus)* produces a chattering high-pitched piping. The Bushy-crested Hornbills can sound like a colony of squabbling seagulls which have lost their way to the sea.

Hornbills often have large, decorative processes (known as casques) above their bills, which accounts for their name. However, only in the Helmeted Hornbill is the casque solid, and this was formerly an item of forest trade known as hornbill ivory. In some parts of Sabah it was believed that the wearer of a ring or locket made from the casque would afford protection against any sort of poison. The well-developed casque in a few other species is hollow, and thus not the burden it would appear to be in flight. Hornbills are in fact quite graceful flyers, sweeping overhead with a whooshing noise caused by their large wings.

Rhinoceros Hornbill (*Buceros rhinoceros*) pauses on a tree branch high in the canopy. *(Photo: M. Strange)*

The dark forest understorey

Once your eyes have adjusted to the lower light levels of the forest understorey, you will, with a little luck, see a large variety of plants and animals. One of the first likely encounters, even if not the most pleasant, is the forest leech. Leeches are predatory blood-sucking animals which are found in the humid forest understorey. Watch a green, orange and black striped Painted Leech (*Haemadipsa picta*), which a moment ago was perched motionless on a leaf beside the forest trail, but now loops across the intervening vegetation on adhesive suckers at either end of its body, trying to locate you from your body heat.

Leech bites are messy as the anticoagulant which the leech injects when it bites prevents blood clotting. If you are unlucky enough to find a leech on yourself, it is perfectly safe to pull off the leech in the middle of its meal. Contrary to popular belief, it does not leave behind its mouth parts. Leeches do not carry any disease, unlike ticks and mosquitoes, but be careful, as the irritation from leech bites can continue for several days afterwards. Try not to scratch the area as you may introduce a troublesome secondary infection into the wound.

Fungi are also abundant in the dark humid atmosphere of the forest floor. Often, one will find many showy, colourful mushrooms and toadstools sprouting from the forest floor, fallen branches or from rotting logs. Look more closely at a piece of decayed wood with a toadstool sprouting from it, and you may be able to see the thin strands of fungal tissue that have spread into the wood, feeding on the carbon-rich compounds. Fungi are called saprophytes as they obtain all their nutrients from decaying or dead plant material. By their action, fungi decompose and recycle nutrients which would otherwise be unavailable to living plants.

Some fungi associate with the roots of plants (the root-fungus structures are called mycorrhizae) and perform other crucial functions for living plants in the forest. Orchid seeds, for example, will not germinate until invaded by certain types of mycorrhizal fungi. Mycorrhizal fungi also form associations with the roots of many trees, including dipterocarps. One type of fungus forms sheath-like structures around the fine roots, helping to increase the absorptive surface area that takes up nutrients into the roots. The tree, in return, provides the fungus with sugars and complex compounds essential for fungal growth. Dipterocarp trees are known to

The brightly coloured Painted Leech (*Haemadipsa picta*), which is more common on low vegetation, does not inject an anaesthetic and therefore gives a sharp stinging bite, hence its other name, "Tiger Leech". Its relative, the brown Common Land Leech (*Haemadipsa zeylanica*), is mostly found on the forest floor and has a painless bite, as it injects an anaesthetic with the anticoagulant. *(Photo: K.M. Wong)*

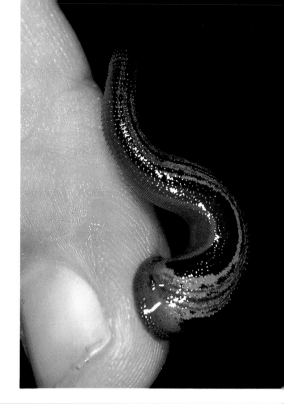

The coral fungus (*Ramaria* sp.) displays an antler-like assemblage of branches in its fruiting body, just one of the many amazing shapes encountered in the world of fungi. *(Photo: C.L. Chan)*

The delicate, hairy cup fungus, *Cookeina tricholoma*, on a decaying twig.
(*Photo: A.Y.C. Chung*)

have mycorrhizal roots and it has been shown that seedlings with the fungus can grow several times faster than seedlings lacking the fungus.

You will notice many different types of fern on your walk, most of which also prefer the dark, humid conditions of the forest understorey. Ferns can be found gracing the forest floor, the trunks of trees and the rocks at stream banks. Filmy ferns (family Hymenophyllaceae) in particular, grow only in moist places as their leaves are only one-cell to several cells thick and so require a humid environment or they will desiccate.

Ferns, pitcher plants and orchids

Other types of fern grow as epiphytes in much drier conditions, anchored firmly to a tree trunk or wedged in at the base of a large branch. Some ferns found in tree crowns, like the Bird's Nest Fern (*Asplenium nidus*), are so large that water and plant matter collects in the base of their leaves, acting as a reservoir of moisture and nutrients for the fern. Such places are sometimes used by frogs and insects as breeding sites.

Pitcher plants (*Nepenthes* spp.) are another group of plants that have adopted a different way of acquiring nutrients. They are common in montane and heath forests, which have soils rather poor in nutrients, growing on the ground as well as low down on the vegetation. Pitcher plants can also be found growing in lowland rain forest, some climbing to the crowns of canopy trees. The leaf tips of pitcher plants are modified to form elegant, colourful red and green cups which contain a fluid rich in digestive enzymes. Any invertebrates unwary enough to fall in are slowly dissolved, providing essential nutrients such as nitrogen to the plant.

The orchids (family Orchidaceae), which attract interest because of their pretty or unusual flowers, also include many epiphytic species. Many epiphytic orchids grow high up in the branches of tall forest trees but some prefer the darker conditions of the forest understorey or forest floor. Some orchid species are saprophytic and have no leaves, obtaining all their nutrients from the soil and decaying plant matter in the leaf litter. There are more than 1,400 species of orchid in 147 genera found in the rain forests of Borneo.

Medusa's Orchid (*Bulbophyllum medusae*), with tightly clustered flowers that bear long, flowing flower sepals, recalling the snaky locks of the mythological Medusa's head. *(Photo: C.L. Chan)*

Delicate blooms of Swan's Necklace Orchid (*Coelogyne swaniana*), held on a pendulous inflorescence. *(Photo: C.L. Chan)*

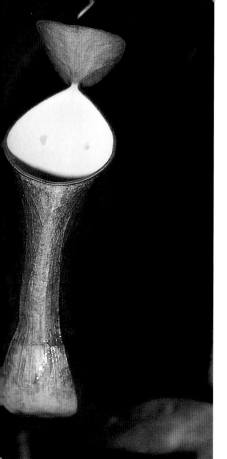

Nepenthes reinwardtiana, a lowland rain forest pitcher-plant species. *(Photo: A. Lamb)*

Sweetly scented, mottled flowers of the Elephant's Ear Orchid (*Phalaenopsis gigantea*). *(Photo: C.L. Chan)*

The terrestrial orchid, *Calanthe zollingeri*, with elegant white flowers, is in Borneo known only in the lowland forest of the Danum Valley in Sabah. *(Photo: C.L. Chan)*

Small forest streams

Small mammals that are active by day include the treeshrews (family Tupaiidae). They are sometimes seen foraging for fruits and insects in low streamside vegetation. Treeshrews are often mistaken for squirrels but they are actually more closely related to primates. Five of the eight species of treeshrews occurring in Borneo are endemic to the island.

Some forest birds also frequent small streams, so if you sit quietly by one you may be lucky enough to spot some birds, such as the beautiful White-crowned Forktail (*Enicurus leschenaulti*), searching among stones for insects or flitting about restlessly near the water's edge.

The Giant Squirrel (*Ratufa affinis*), Borneo's largest. *(Photo: M. Strange)*

If you look closely at the surface of the stream you may see some aquatic bugs, pond skaters and water boatmen (order Hemiptera), dancing around. These bugs spend most of their adult lives on the water surface catching other insects which fall onto the water and are trapped by its surface tension. A beautiful iridescent gauzy-winged dragonfly (order Odonata) may flash its wings above the still surface of a temporary pool, occasionally darting down to lay eggs in the water.

A school of silvery fish might glint in the sun as they swim past, swishing their tails to disturb plant and animal debris on the stream bottom which is then devoured. A small soft-shelled turtle, which at first may be mistaken for a rock, may poke out its head, expand its long neck and snatch up small fish or freshwater prawns as they swim past.

Forest growth and decay

While walking in the forest you will notice that the trees are not uniformly spaced apart. The vegetation is a mixture of plants of different ages and sizes, scattered about without any particular design and very much a consequence of an uneven distribution of seeds and other propagules, and of the development of the forest being cyclic. Forest development has three major growth phases that, even in a small area of forest, can be found growing together like a mosaic or a crazy patchwork quilt. One of the first phases of growth is found in forest gaps, often created by treefalls, where there is much light reaching the forest floor. Here various animals may also be seen.

Cold-blooded animals such as reptiles are sluggish in the early morning and rely partly on heat from the sun's rays to provide energy sufficient for movement. A familiar forest reptile found sunning itself in bright sunny spots on fallen trees or decaying logs is the burnished coppery-coloured Rough Skink, *Mabuya rudis*. A characteristic sound as you walk along a forest trail or through a sunny gap is the skitter of a disturbed basking skink disappearing into the forest-floor litter.

Other types of reptile such as snakes may also be seen in sunny areas but they are generally difficult to spot as they are secretive and well camouflaged. There are around one hundred different snakes in Borneo, but only the King Cobra (*Ophiophagus hannah*) and Black Cobra (*Najah sumatrana*) are likely to inflict a bite fatal to humans. Sabah's lowland

Structure of the three phases of forest regeneration

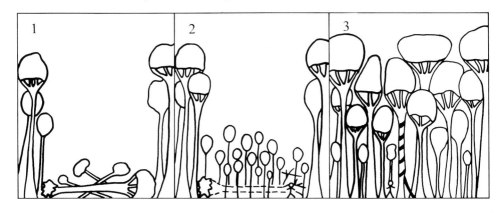

1. The Gap Phase. A gap created by a recently dead tree fall, is an open, sunny and hot area having no understorey or forest canopy.
2. The Building Phase. The forest understorey is a dense stand of saplings and liana growth, with a low forest canopy.
3. Mature Phase forest has a more open understorey, dominated by large trees, a high forest canopy and large-stemmed lianas extending into the canopy.

When a large tree falls, it can also bring down other trees and liana stems with it, creating a gap in the forest canopy. *(Photo: E.J.F. Campbell)*

The Rough Skink (*Mabuya rudis*) basking on a dead palm leaf in a sunny spot on the forest floor. *(Photo: R. Stuebing)*

Master of camouflage, the Green Fence Lizard (*Bronchocoela cristatella*) can vary its body colour through shades of green and brown to suit its place of rest. *(Photo: C.L. Chan)*

The long-legged centipede, of the genus *Scutigera*, moves swiftly despite its cumbersome appearance. Carnivorous in diet, it feeds on crickets and a variety of other insects. *(Photo: C.L. Chan)*

The "tractor" millipede. Millipedes differ from centipedes in having two pairs of legs on most body segments, instead of one. *(Photo: C.L. Chan)*

Looking like their fossil namesake, Trilobite beetle (*Duliticola paradoxa*) females retain their larval form even when sexually mature. *(Photo: C.L. Chan)*

forest snakes come in every hue from the beautiful, green, pencil-thin Oriental or Grass-green Whip Snake (*Ahaetulla prasina*) with its bright blue tongue, to the plain brown or olive King Cobra, the world's largest poisonous snake that can reach 3.5 m long. Even if snakes are accidentally encountered, they nearly always slither away into the undergrowth rather than confront, as long as they are not challenged or provoked. It is well to note that sometimes disturbed snakes can convincingly feign death.

If you examine and peel off the bark of a fallen decaying tree, you may uncover various kinds of invertebrate, i.e. animals with no "backbones". Insects such as Longhorn beetles (family Cerambycidae), easily recognised by their long antennae, lay their eggs in the bark of living trees. Other common invertebrates include trilobite beetles, woodlice, centipedes, millipedes and snails. All these invertebrates assist the

Old, sculptured termite nest at the base of a forest tree. *(Photo: E.J.F. Campbell)*

recycling of plant and animal matter in forest soils in their various ways.

Centipedes are predatory, fast-moving animals which inject a poison that kills or paralyses their prey. Centipedes should not be touched as they defend themselves vigorously and some can inflict a very painful bite. Millipedes, on the other hand, are inoffensive vegetarians; they move slowly and often forage in the decaying leaf litter of the forest floor or on decaying wood.

Dung beetles (family Scarabaeidae) assist in the decomposition of decaying plant matter in animal dung. Dung-rolling dung beetles have specially shaped back legs which assist in rolling dung into balls which the beetles then bury in the soil along with their eggs. The hatched grubs obtain nourishment from the buried dung.

Two other groups of insects that are important recyclers of nutrients are the ants and termites. Ants are the most abundant insect in the rain forest, and are predators or scavengers of both living and dead plant and animal material. Columns of ants winding their way along the forest floor and surrounding vegetation are a common sight; a scent trail is laid so the ants can find their way back to their nest with their "booty". Termites, unlike ants, are exclusively decomposers of leaves and wood. Some termite species harbour microscopic Protozoa in their intestines which help in the digestion of lignin, the basic stuff of wood. Other termite species culture tiny fungi which digest lignin and cellulose (from leaves) from the termite droppings. Lines of what appears to be soil on wood or leaves often indicate the presence of a termite trail. The "soil" is actually small wood fragments mixed with saliva, used to protect the termites from predators such as ants. Termite nests are made of the same material and can be found under or above ground and attached to or even inside trees. The nests are often constructed in a form characteristic of the species. An old nest which is broken will show the intricate intercommunicating chambers and galleries inside.

The Giant Forest Ant (*Camponotus gigas*), the largest of the forest ant species. The workers can reach 2.5 cm long and are often seen wandering around on the forest floor during the daytime. The queen (shown here) is less frequently encountered. At night, these ants forage in the forest canopy. *(Photo: C.L. Chan)*

The crown of a Menggaris tree (*Koompassia excelsa*), which can grow over 80 m tall. *(Photo: A.Y.C. Chung)*

Sun Bear. (Drawing by Jamal Hassim)

One of the main predators of ants and termites is the Sun Bear (*Helarctos malayanus*), which uses its large, powerful claws to rip open soil and wood. Its long sticky tongue then "mops" up the ants and termites inside. Sun bears also love the contents of honey bee nests and will go to great lengths in search of nests, even climbing trees.

The nests of wild honey bees tend to be built in the highest possible parts of trees, out of reach to most predators like the sun bear. A favoured site is in the crown of the Menggaris tree (*Koompassia excelsa*), a leguminous tree found scattered throughout lowland forest. Menggaris trees are often as high as, or even higher than, the tallest dipterocarp trees; some reach over 80 m high, making them the tallest tree species recorded in Borneo. Their beautiful silvery grey trunks and bright green, almost feathery crowns make them easy to recognise. Although wild honey bee nests made in Menggaris tree crowns may be safe from sun bears, they are not safe from humans, for sometimes, local people build ingenious ladders of wooden pegs up the trunk to harvest the honey. If you see a tree with scars in a line up the trunk, you can be sure that someone has climbed it and now lays claim to that particular tree.

THE MID-DAY LULL

By mid-morning the forest is much quieter. Most of the birds have stopped singing and are now foraging for food. Usually, different bird species hunt separately but sometimes you will notice the return of bird chatter as a mixed flock of birds moves through the forest near you. This mixed flock is a hunting association of many different species, some looking for fruits and nectar, others for insects. As a group, they scour the forest at every level from the forest floor to the canopy and present an ideal opportunity for some extensive bird watching. A mixed flock may include species of sunbirds, leafbirds, flycatchers, drongos, jays, bulbuls and babblers.

Barbets (family Capitonidae) are birds that never seem to tire of their own voice; even at mid-day their loud *took..took..turook..* calls can be heard everywhere. Barbets are shy relatives of woodpeckers and use their broad powerful bills to bore nest holes in trees. Barbets have bright green bodies and colourful heads with red, blue and yellow markings but are usually difficult to see as they spend most of their time in the forest canopy.

Punctuating the silence intermittently throughout the day are the calls from Sabah's largest and most spectacular ground-dwelling pheasant, the Great Argus (*Argusianus argus*). Both males and females make loud calls - *tuwau, tuwau, tuwau* - but the breeding male also has a very striking long call which it uses to attract females. The long call starts with a number of clear, single notes repeated many times, the last few notes rising in pitch and increasing in tempo. Made from its "dancing ground", which is a circle 4-5 m wide kept scrupulously clean of forest floor litter, the call carries a great distance through the forest and is one of the most evocative and characteristic sounds in lowland rain forest. The courtship display involves the erection of the male's long tail feathers into a concave fan, of which the brown, cream and white feathers are patterned with intricate dots and lines. The courtship dance is rarely seen and only performed once. In western Sabah, the male Argus's tail feathers are much prized by the Murut people for use in their headdresses.

Green Broadbill (*Calyptomena viridis*) feeding on figs in the lowland forest.
(*Photo: Frans Lanting / Minden Pictures*)

Hooved forest animals

Other animals that may shatter the peace of the forest are two species of barking deer, the Common Barking Deer (*Muntiacus muntjak*) and the Bornean Yellow Muntjac (*Muntiacus atherodes*). The adults give short, loud barking calls when disturbed and can startle if they call close by. The barking signals to predators that they have been spotted, letting them know it may be a waste of time for them to stalk the deer. In dense forest, the barking is more effective than deploying a visual distress signal, such as a tail flash employed by some other deer, which may not be clearly seen.

Two other deer which may be seen during the day are the Greater Mouse-deer (*Tragulus napu*) and Lesser Mouse-deer (*Tragulus javanicus*). Mouse-deer, standing only 20 cm high and smallest of the forest deer, are very timid and shy. If disturbed, they will run into the undergrowth but do not usually move far. If you follow very quietly, you may be able to see this dainty little deer foraging on the forest floor. In Malay folk tales the mouse-deer, or *kancil*, always gets the better of the bigger and stronger animals by superior cunning.

Another ungulate species you may come across is the Bearded Pig (*Sus barbatus*), which will crash off into the undergrowth with a grunt or two. If female, she may have been accompanied by a litter of piglets. Young piglets have pale spots and stripes to help camouflage them in the vegetation. Bearded pigs are hosts to numerous ticks which can carry tick fever or scrub typhus and are difficult to remove from the body. Do not walk through or sit near any unnatural piles of leaves and twigs, which could be nests made by bearded pigs.

Sow of the Bearded Pig (*Sus barbatus*), so named for the bushy tufts of bristles on either side of the snout. *(Photo: M. Heydon)*

The Asian Two-Horned or Sumatran Rhinoceros (*Dicerorhinus sumatrensis*), once more widespread, is now only found in eastern Sabah, the Ulu Baram area, in Sarawak, and possibly adjacent parts of Kalimantan. Over thousands of years, hunting by humans for their meat and horn, which is believed by some to possess medicinal properties, has reduced their numbers considerably. Although a protected species, rhinos still fall prey to illegal poaching. Only about fifty are thought to remain in Sabah, where most inhabit an area of the Dent Peninsula and scattered populations occur between the Segama and Kinabatangan Rivers. Rhinos are shy, elusive, solitary animals, active from late afternoon to early

Sambar Deer (*Cervus unicolor*), the largest forest deer, is found in open areas of forest such as river banks and forest edges. These deer are more active at night, although one can occasionally be seen during the day. (*Photo: A. Lamb*)

morning but have been occasionally seen during the day. They apparently prefer to eat mature leaves and twigs from a wide variety of plants, rather than more succulent plant shoots. Rhino presence is often only indicated by their distinctive footprints with three clear toe marks or the deep score marks in the sides of wallows made by their horns. Their wallows are sometimes encountered in lowland forest though it is not really known why rhinos use wallows. They may be good places to keep cool during the hottest part of the day or the mud in the wallow may keep off skin parasites such as flies and ticks.

Sumatran Rhinoceros. (Drawing by Jamal Hassim)

Flowering and fruiting trees

With such a profusion of plant life in the forest, you might expect, at any time of the year, to find many trees flowering or fruiting but this is often not the case. Although the forest microclimate is stable, many tree species reproduce only at certain times of the year with all the adult trees of each species reproducing simultaneously; this event is a "mini" mast fruiting. In the lowland forest of Sabah, mast fruiting occurs from around April to September, depending on the forest area, and can be quite patchy in occurrence.

Some rattans, such as this *Calamus ornatus*, have edible fruits. *(Photo: A. Lamb)*

The wild relatives of the nutmeg genus *Myristica*, including many species in lowland forest, similarly produce seeds clothed in a finely dissected, brightly coloured mace. *(Photo: E.J.F. Campbell)*

A flowering emergent dipterocarp tree in the lowland forest. (*Photo: Frans Lanting / Minden Pictures*)

This patchy fruiting may partly explain why certain animals such as bearded pig and orang utan may not be seen for weeks in one area but then suddenly turn up in large numbers. Both these species are partly migratory, and can follow fruiting events over surprisingly long distances. Pigs, especially, are known to range tens of kilometers in search of fruiting trees.

At intervals of five to eight or nine years, a major fruiting event (a "mega" mast fruiting) occurs throughout Borneo's lowland rain forest. During these episodes, the emergent dipterocarps and most other canopy and understorey trees flower and then fruit simultaneously; the forest floor becomes littered with many different types of fruit. The "trigger" that brings on such a mast fruiting is still not well understood, although many suggestions have been put forward, including drought, unnaturally heavy rainfall and even an increase in sunspot activity.

Bunches of nearly mature, bright red, two-winged fruits cover the crown of a dipterocarp tree (*Dipterocarpus* sp.). *(Photo: A. Lamb)*

Figs - the trees of life

During times when there is little fruit, fig trees (*Ficus* spp.) become important for many fruit-eating animals, as unlike most other trees, many of them bear fruit frequently and at different times throughout the year. Figs owe part of their strange reproductive behaviour to their dependence on tiny fig wasps for the pollination of their flowers which are enclosed inside a fleshy outer coat.

The mouth of the developing fruit is penetrated by a female fig wasp which lays one egg in the ovary of each flower until her supply of eggs is exhausted and she dies. The eggs develop and are nourished by the fig walls until they hatch. The adult fig wasps then mate, the males die and the females leave the fig in search of a new fig which is just developing. On their way out of the fig mouth, the female wasps pick up pollen from male flowers which is transferred to female flowers in the new figs which they enter.

Figs are nutritious and sustain many animals. Their often bright colours are attractive, and each fig structure bears innumerable tiny flowers or fruits within.
(*Photo: A. Lamb*)

How a strangling fig develops

1. Birds and arboreal mammals which eat the figs, drop seeds on the branches of forest trees where they grow into epiphytic bushes. The bush develops strong roots that encircle the host.

2. The fig's own roots gradually grow downwards, where they anchor in the ground, thickening in the process. Side roots grow around the trunk, joining up with other roots, and sometimes, aerial roots grow straight down into the soil from various heights.

3. The host trunk becomes enveloped in a basket of fig roots and the fig's foliage spreads widely through the tree's crown. The trunk cannot grow outwards, crushed against the fig roots, and is gradually "ringed" until it dies. The dead tree rots away over many years, leaving the fig tree with its unusual, often hollow, shape.

Figs have more variety of growth, leaf and fruit form than any other group of Bornean trees. They can be scrambling climbers, thick-stemmed lianas, epiphytes and the most bizarre form, the strangling fig. Strangling fig trees are trees whose trunks are composed of a basketwork of interlacing and joined roots.

Fig trees in fruit are usually easy to find in the forest and such trees offer unrivalled opportunities for mammal and bird watching. If you encounter a fruiting fig tree, find a concealed spot with a good view of the crown and wait quietly. Throughout the day, a number of animals will come to feed.

The best known, and probably the most appealing of Borneo's primates, the Orang Utan (*Pongo pygmaeus*) will probably visit as they are extremely fond of fig fruits. Although orang utans are generally solitary, unlike gibbons and other monkeys which are found in family groups, they occasionally move around with other individuals. The orang utans move slowly and deliberately around in the fig branches, looking for ripe fruit and have been seen to chase off gibbons who have to wait until the orang utans have had their fill.

Long-tailed Macaque (*Macaca fascicularis*) at one of its feeding stations, a strangling fig (*Ficus benjamina*) in fruit. *(Photo: M. Strange)*

At full development, the pillar roots of a strangling fig (*Ficus benjamina*) appear to mark out some kind of territory. *(Photo: C.L. Chan)*

Mother and baby orang utan. *(Photo: Frans Lanting / Minden Pictures)*

Every evening, individual orang utans make a new nest in the crook of a tree's branches, generally near a fruiting tree. They build their nest by bending and stacking leafy branches into a small platform. If you glance up into the forest canopy now and again when you are on your walk, you may see some old nests which are a mess of dead leaves and twigs. These nests can often indicate where and in what numbers orang utans occur.

Fruiting fig trees may also attract up to twenty hornbills feeding at one time, quite a disincentive for other, smaller, bird species to visit. Asian Fairy Bluebirds, bulbuls, broadbills and pigeons are just some of the birds which will visit fig trees during the day.

It is inevitable that, with all this feeding activity, some of the ripe figs will drop to the ground. If you visit the tree at night, you may come across some of Sabah's smaller animals eating the fallen figs, including the mouse-deer, civets and even tortoises.

A Spiny Tortoise (*Heosemys spinosa*), one of a variety found in lowland rain forest. (Drawing by Jamal Hassim)

River coursing through lush lowland rain forest. *(Photo: A. Lamb)*

FOREST STREAMS AND RIVERS

Where rivers and streams exist in the dense lowland forest, the canopy is broken and more light reaches the ground. Many of the tree species which grow along rivers have short crooked trunks and drooping branches dangling above the moving water. Fruits of many riverine trees float and are dispersed by water.

Often seen flitting along the open bright river banks and sunny forest streams are many of Sabah's beautifully coloured butterflies looking for flower nectar and mineral salts. The Birdwing butterflies (family Papilionidae), with black markings and yellow, white, blue or green patches, may be the most striking. The Rajah Brooke's Birdwing (*Trogonoptera brookiana*) is the forest's most magnificent butterfly, with its 18-cm wingspan. The Tree Nymph butterfly (*Idea iasonia*) resembles a translucent, polka-dot bow tie, fluttering and gliding at forest edges and in sunny patches of the forest understorey.

Common Bluebottle (*Graphium sarpedon*) congregating with other butterflies on a damp stream bank. They probe their long proboscis in the sand to drink the mineral salts. (*Photo: A. Lamb*)

At dawn, forest and river become visible again as the shroud of mist begins to dissipate. *(Photo: W.M. Poon)*

Birdwing butterfly (*Troides amphrysus*), newly emerged from its chrysalis. *(Photo: C.L. Chan)*

Gaudily coloured as a signal to ward off predators, a moth caterpillar continues its feeding relentlessly. *(Photo: C.L. Chan)*

Delicate threads suspend a Birdwing's intricate chrysalis. *(Photo: C.L. Chan)*

Caterpillars of the Palm King butterfly (*Amathusia* sp.) survive solely on a diet of palm leaves. *(Photo: C.L. Chan)*

The caterpillars of butterflies can be equally attractive with brightly coloured dots, stripes, spines or long fine hairs. These hairs, often tipped with poison, are a defence against predators, and can cause a nasty rash on human skin. If a hairy caterpillar accidentally drops on your skin, brush it off in the direction it is travelling so the poisonous tips do not break off.

Riverine plants

At stream and river banks, one can see substantial numbers of lianas or climbing plants. Lianas climb other plants to reach the higher light levels in the forest canopy. At river banks the higher light levels and disturbance due to the periodic flooding of the river allow lianas to proliferate, giving the forest the appearance of a leafy-blanketed jungle.

Begonias often have attractive colours and patterns on the leaves, which may enhance light capture at the level of the forest floor, where light intensities are low and different component wavelengths predominate. *(Photo: C.L. Chan)*

Abundant light on river banks encourages a profuse growth of shrubs and creepers, in great contrast to an often thinner undergrowth beneath forest canopy. *(Photo: Frans Lanting / Minden Pictures)*

Large and bright yellow bloom of the *simpoh* (*Dillenia excelsa*), common by river banks. *(Photo: A.Y.C. Chung)*

Rattan (family Palmae), a special group of climbing palms, also flourish along rivers. Beware, they have whip-like appendages with many fine hooks which are used to facilitate climbing and can just as easily catch hold of clothing and skin as other plants. Rattan is a locally important non-timber forest product. The strong pliable stems are used for making many types of furniture. Rattans are now being planted as a crop in disturbed forest areas and are becoming an important commercial forest product in Sabah.

Another important group supplying an important local non-timber product which can be found along rivers is bamboo (family Gramineae). Bamboos have hollow woody stems and they are used extensively in rural areas for many purposes such as building materials for housing, fences, poles, blow pipes and even musical instruments. In the past the hollow stems were also used as water containers and for cooking rice while the tender shoots are still a local delicacy.

Whereas in the forest understorey there is little light and therefore few herbs present on the forest floor, the sunnier conditions of river banks allow denser patches of herbs to occur. Begonias and ginger plants, two types of common herbs, are often quite conspicuous because of their attractive flowers and unusual leaves. Begonias (family Begoniaceae) come in many forms from small, squat rosettes with glossy green, variegated or iridescent blue-green leaves to large many-stemmed plants up to 1 m tall with all parts covered in long silky hairs. There are around 60 species found in Sabah.

Ginger plants (family Zingiberaceae) are equally varied in shape and size. Gingers vary from the delicate little *Globba*, with tiny contorted orange or red flowers at the end of a short leafy stem, to the gigantic torch gingers (*Etlingera* spp.). Many are quite spectacular in flower, with the leafy shoots towering above one's head and large, showy red to white flowers in clumps at the ground or on stalks up to 1 m tall. Many members of the ginger family have aromatic parts. Ginger and turmeric come from the rhizomes, and scented cardamom fruits or flowers are used locally to flavour special dishes such as "sambal" and "laksa".

Torch Ginger (*Etlingera elatior*), with large, showy pink or red flowers on stalks up to 1 m high. The petals of the flower are used in some fiery, spicy local dishes. *(Photo: E.J.F. Campbell)*

Boisenbergia aurantiaca is an attractive ginger recently discovered and described from Sabah's Danum Valley. *(Photo: E.J.F. Campbell)*

Common birds of rivers

In the sunnier habitat of river banks you may see small brightly coloured birds such as leafbirds, flycatchers, flowerpeckers, and sunbirds flying across the river or flitting through the vegetation. Wild banana plants (*Musa* spp.) are a favoured spot of spider-hunters (family Nectariniidae). Although they are mainly insect feeders, they also feed on the nectar of the banana flowers. Spider-hunters build their nests suspended from under the surface of large horizontal leaves such as those of wild bananas and gingers.

Brilliantly coloured, dagger-beaked Kingfishers (family Alcedinidae) may flash past along rivers looking for fish, or sit motionless on an exposed perch overhanging the river bank. Unlike European kingfishers, some Asian species live in the forest, far from water, feeding on insects such as beetles, crickets, grasshoppers and cicadas.

In open forest areas, such as along river banks and at forest edges, one may hear the plaintive high-pitched whistling calls of a Crested Serpent-eagle (*Spilornis cheela*), which soars high above the river, looking for a snake or other potential prey.

Rufous-backed Kingfisher (*Ceyx rufidorsa*), a jewel among kingfishers. *(Photo: M. Strange)*

Common river animals

While walking beside a forested river near Sabah's coast, keep a look out for the largest of Sabah's monkeys, the Proboscis Monkey (*Nasalis larvatus*). Although they are mainly confined to mangrove forest and coastal habitats these monkeys can be found living hundreds of kilometres upstream along fresh-water rivers. The best time to see proboscis monkeys is in the early morning or late afternoon, when they gather along the river banks, looking for succulent young leaves and shoots, or searching for a

A spider-hunter rests amid drinking nectar from the flowers of the wild banana, *Musa beccarii*. *(Photo: K.M. Wong)*

Decorated in vividly coloured plumes, a Chestnut-breasted Malkoha (*Phaenicophaeus curvirostris*) looks warily about its perch. *(Photo: M. Strange)*

new sleeping site. Proboscis monkeys are largely arboreal but will readily swim across rivers.

The Oriental Small-clawed Otter (*Aonyx cinerea*) is sometimes seen along rivers and streams, fishing or eating crabs and other crustaceans. If you come across a well-trampled spot smelling particularly of rotting fish, it may have been an otter's feeding spot. Look for otter faeces, characterised by pieces of crab shells, fish bones and scales. Adult small-clawed otters can sometimes be seen frolicking together with their young.

Predator on the prowl: a Common Monitor Lizard (*Varanus salvator*) roams a river bank. *(Photo: M. Strange)*

Proboscis monkey.

The reptile most often seen beside rivers is probably the Common or Water Monitor Lizard (*Varanus salvator*). Water monitors instinctively jump into the river at the first sign of disturbance, so listen for a loud splash as you walk along the river. They reach 2 m in length and are scavengers, feeding on carrion but also any live animal prey. They can even be seen looking for food scraps at human habitations. Young monitors are green with yellow spots whereas adults are olive green and therefore more difficult to see. There is also the Rough-naped Monitor Lizard (*Varanus rudicollis*) found in the forest, but it is quite rare and you are most unlikely to see it.

The other reptile you might spot near rivers is the Reticulated Python (*Python reticulatus*), which can grow to a length of 9 m. Pythons are not poisonous snakes, but kill their prey by constriction with strong coils of their body. Pythons are also expert swimmers and their brown colouration, with a network of black yellow-edged lines, help camouflage them against the litter of the forest floor.

Sabah's lowland forest rivers contain about 60 species of fish including catfish, eels, carp and gouramy. The most common group are the carp (family Cyprinidae) some of which make good eating. The Giant Goramy (*Osphronemus laticlavius*) caught in larger rivers, is

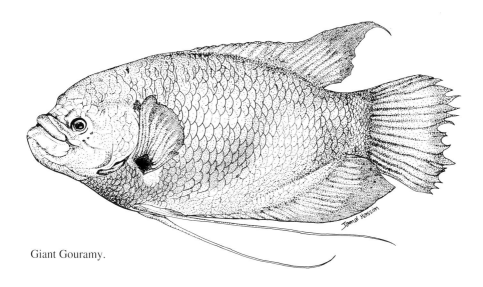

Giant Gouramy.

kept in tanks by local people who believe this fish will prevent bad luck and unhappiness from entering the home. It can weigh up to several kilograms and is also an important food fish.

The Oriental Small-clawed Otter (*Aonyx fascicularis*), a swift and agile swimmer, is sometimes seen along Sabah's freshwater rivers and streams. *(Photo: A. Lamb)*

Late-afternoon birds

In the afternoon there is a lull in forest noises, except for the occasional bird calls from barbets or a Plaintive Cuckoo (*Cacomantis merulinus*), the most common lowland cuckoo. This cuckoo's song is quite mournful, hence its name. Its alternative name, "Brain-fever Bird" is given for the persistence with which it can repeat its call.

The Common or Greater Coucal (*Centropus sinensis*), another bird with a rather mournful call, is common in disturbed lowland forest such as along large rivers. Its dull booming call, often running down and then up the scale, although melodious, is rather doleful. Coucals may be seen prowling about river banks in the late afternoon or on forest edges, foraging for grasshoppers, other insects, snails, seeds and fruit.

Plaintive Cuckoo. (Drawing by Jamal Hassim)

AROUND DUSK

At dusk one will notice the arrival of swallows and swifts, swooping down low over the river, having a last drink. Swifts (family Apodidae) spend all their active lives on the wing, catching flying insects as their sole food. Insectivorous bats will start to emerge from their roosts and, if you are very lucky, the incredibly fast Bat Hawk (*Machaeramphus alcinus*) will appear to catch unwary bats before dark. Bat hawks live an easy life around bat caves but are also found roosting in old hollow trees.

Fruit bats can also be found roosting in riverine trees, and the Large Flying Fox (*Pteropus vampyrus*), with a wingspan of 1.5 m, is the largest of Sabah's bats. It does not, as its scientific name suggests, feed on blood but rather on flower nectar and fruits. It helps pollinate night opening flowers of many forest trees, including Durian (*Durio* spp.), and will sometimes fly long distances to feed. One roost tree may, on a single night, contain hundreds of flying foxes draping the branches and quarrelling noisily.

Green Cicada (*Dundubia vaginata*), one of several species whose chorus permeates the rain forest at dusk. (*Photo: C.L. Chan*)

Cantor's Roundleaf Bat (*Hipposideros galeritus*), an insectivorous forest bat which roosts in caves. (*Photo: R. Stuebing*)

Cicadas (family Cicadidae), large sap-sucking insects, can be heard calling intermittently throughout the day but at dusk and dawn their calls vie for attention. Cicadas start calling in response to a light intensity trigger and as a different point of light intensity is reached, new species will start calling, until all the cicadas in the vicinity seem to be calling in every musical pitch from base to highest falsetto. The noise cicadas make is created by the vibration of a membrane across cavities in the sides of the body which act as a sounding box. The so-called six o'clock cicada gives the loudest and weirdest call at around six every evening and morning, a long drawn out *waaaaah, wa...h, wa...h, wa...h, wa...h, wa...h.*

Praying mantids (order Mantodea) are predators and use mimicry to deceive potential prey; this includes the Dead Leaf Mantid *(Deroplatys dessicata)* which, as the common name implies, mimics a dead leaf to deceive unwary insects.

An attractive Flower Mantid (*Hymenopus coronatus*), when perched among white flowers is a deadly surprise to an unwary visiting insect. *(Photo: C.L. Chan)*

The predator lies in wait: almost indistinguishable from the forest-floor litter, the Dead-leaf Mantid (*Deroplatys dessicata*) assumes a motionless but deadly stance, poised to capture its prey. *(Photo: C.L. Chan)*

A NIGHT WALK IN THE FOREST

Armed only with a large torch light and spare batteries, one can explore the forest at night on foot. By torch light, all the trees, shrubs and herbs stand out in pale relief from the darkness of the surrounding forest. Small misty drops of moisture drift through the light beam and tiny, shiny eyes peer out from the vegetation. If you look closely you will discover that some of these eyes belong to spiders of many shapes and forms. Some of the spiders with big eyes are jumping spiders (family Saltacidae) which do not spin webs but actively hunt at night using their better eyesight and binocular vision.

The Buffy Fish-owl (*Ketupa ketupa*) includes fish, frogs and crustaceans in its diet. It is an unusual owl in that it can be seen hunting during the day at forest edges and river banks. (*Photo: W.M. Poon*)

Mating in the File-eared Frog (*Polypedates otilophus*). The smaller male climbs on the back of the female and clasps her body with his limbs. The foam nest is attached to low vegetation, overhanging water. *(Photo: R. Stuebing)*

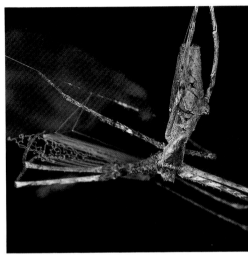

A new one woven each night, the web of the Net-throwing Spider (*Dinopus* sp.) is held in readiness to be cast over an unsuspecting prey. *(Photo: C.L. Chan)*

The Bay Owl (*Phodilus badius*), a beautiful forest owl resembling the European Barn Owl. It nests in hollow trees during the day and forages for small birds, rodents and insects at night. *(Photo: A. Lamb)*

You may also come across some nocturnal birds, such as nightjars, frogmouths or owls. Nightjars can be seen catching insects on the wing but, unlike frogmouths which although look similar, forage for food by picking insects off branches or the ground. Nightjars nest on the ground and when brooding their eggs, the brown mottled plumage affords camouflage and makes them very hard to spot.

At night, an incredible array of frogs make their appearance, some small and brightly pigmented, like the White-toed Tree Frog (*Nyctixalus pictus*). *(Photo: C.L. Chan)*

Once full darkness has fallen, and especially after rain, another noisy chorus begins, the croaking and nattering of male frogs calling out to females. Frogs are highly dependent on water and are unable to move beyond a limited habitat range. They can therefore be seen in dampish areas along rivers and streams, by small pools in forest wallows, or in ditches along road edges. Frogs eat insects and other invertebrates using their long sticky tongue, but large frog species may also eat other frogs, small snakes, and even small birds and mammals. Male frogs are typically smaller than female frogs of the same species.

Things that glow in the dark

As your eyes become accustomed to the darkness, you may notice a faint green or white eerie glow coming from the forest floor. If you shine your torch at the source, you will see that the light is coming from luminous fungi growing on decaying wood. The bioluminescence attracts beetles which eat the fungal caps, collecting fungal spores on their bodies and dispersing the spores when they fly off to visit another piece of decaying wood.

You may also notice some slow-moving, flashing points of light in the forest understorey. These are fire-flies, brownish beetles in the family Lampyridae. Both the immature nymphs, called glow-worms, and the adult fire-flies produce the light, which is caused by symbiotic bacteria in the abdomen. Each species has a particular pattern of flashes which is used to attract a mate. The larvae of fire-flies are predatory and feed largely on snails.

Gliding animals

One of Sabah's most unusual frogs is the Wallace's Tree Frog (*Rhacophorus nigropalmatus*), which lives in the forest canopy and has fully webbed fingers and toes, and smooth-edged flaps of skin along the outer surface of the forearms. This enables it to glide from one tree crown to another, only coming down to the forest floor to breed.

Some reptiles, such as the Paradise Tree Snake (*Chrysopelea paradisi*), can also move from tree to tree without having to come down to the ground. Flying tree snakes can hollow the underside of their body so that a cushion of air is trapped to give them lift. By moving through the air in a ziz-zag fashion, they are able to glide like a floating pocket handkerchief. Tree snakes are also expert climbers, slithering up the vertical trunks of trees.

The nocturnal flying squirrels can also glide from tree to tree, by extending flaps of skin between the front and back limbs, and in "flight" can look just like a large tea tray, or a frying pan with its tail for a handle! Another nocturnal flying mammal which can be mistaken for a flying squirrel is the Flying Lemur (*Cynocephalus variegatus*). Unlike flying squirrels which have long visible tails, the tail of the flying lemur is joined to the hind limbs by extra membranes so the tail is not visible, making it kite-shaped.

Clinging to the side of a tree, a Flying Lemur (*Cynocephalus variegatus*) takes a rest from its gliding forays through the rain forest. *(Photo: M. Strange)*

Other nocturnal mammals

Although hedgehogs do not occur in Asia, they have a peculiar relative living in the Bornean lowland forest. The Moonrat (*Echinosorex gymnurus*) has a long snout, with very small, sharp teeth used to chew earthworms and insects. It also has a characteristic pungent odour reminiscent of burnt coffee, which probably serves as a warning that it is not worth eating.

Another unusual mammal with a long snout is the Pangolin or Scaly Anteater (*Manis javanica*). The long claws on the forefeet are used to burrow and tear down soil and wood to expose ant and termite nests on which it exclusively feeds. Pangolins have a small narrow mouth which cannot bite, but a long, thin sticky tongue is used to lick up the nest contents.

The Moonrat (*Echinosorex gymnurus*), almost the size of a domestic cat, has an almost naked tail and a body covered in shaggy, white or cream-coloured hair. (*Photo: A. Lamb*)

Many mammals not necessarily thought of as habitually nocturnal are, in fact, most active at night, or around dawn and dusk. One example is the Asian Elephant (*Elephas maximus*), the largest of Sabah's mammals which, like the Sumatran rhino, has become quite rare. Elephants are now only found between the Labuk River in northeastern Sabah and Darvel Bay in the east. Their numbers are decreasing rapidly with loss of habitat and, recently, poaching. Elephants travel in matriarchal herds of between three and forty individuals, although occasionally a lone adult male may be encountered. Grasses, palm shoots, climbing bamboos, and the stems of bananas and gingers form the main part of their diet. Elephants are most at home in disturbed, secondary forest but oil-palm plantation owners are wary of them as they appear to relish the young, tender hearts of the oil-palms. A herd of elephants can cause considerable damage to a plantation, one individual being known to demolish 200 palm trees in a single night!

Like the sun bear, Asian elephants are unpredictable and should be treated with respect.

Civets are quite often seen at night, especially the Common Palm Civet (*Paradoxurus hermaphroditus*) and the Malay Civet (*Viverra tangalunga*). Civets are omnivorous and can often be seen in forest clearings and edges foraging for fruits, insects and small vertebrates such as birds and reptiles.

If you are really lucky, you may encounter one of Sabah's five species of wild cat. The Clouded Leopard (*Neofilis nebulosa*) is the largest cat and has an attractive

Pangolin or Scaly Anteater (*Manis javanica*). Anteaters are the only mammals with overlapping scales rather than hair on their upper body. The scales are composed of consolidated hairs just as is rhinoceros horn. *(Photo: A. Lamb)*

The Slow Loris (*Nycticebus coucang*), a tubby, furry arboreal primate with big brown eyes, searches out smaller animals such as lizards and insects, or pulpy fruits, as food. (*Photo: W.M. Poon*)

pattern of cloud-like markings on the sides of the body. Clouded Leopards are arboreal but in disturbed forest often travel on the ground. Although the Clouded Leopard feeds on pig, deer, monkeys and smaller mammals, it is not actually a very fierce animal and is shy of man. The smallest of the wild cats is the Leopard Cat (*Felis bengalensis*), about the size of a domestic cat and with a reddish- or yellowish-buff coat with black spots over the entire upperparts, including its tail.

The Leopard Cat (*Felis bengalensis*), smallest of the wild cats in Borneo's forests. (*Photo: A. Lamb*)

Western Tarsier (*Tarsius bancanus*), one of the strangest of Sabah's mammals. The soft, furry body is only 13 cm long, with a 20-cm hairless tail, and frog-like feet. The eyes, although larger than those of the Slow Loris, give off a pale pink rather than red eye shine in torch light. (*Photo: A. Lamb*)

Malay Civet (*Viverra tangalunga*) on its nocturnal prowl. *(Photo: Frans Lanting / Minden Pictures)*

Asian Elephant: mother and calf. (Drawing by C.L. Chan)

Tracks of forest animals

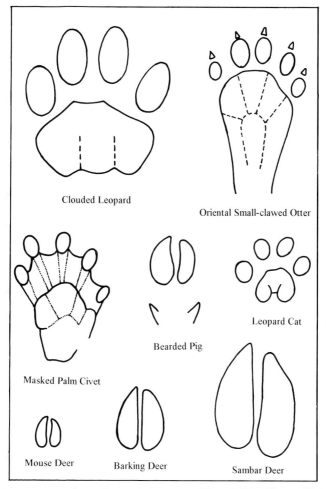

Clouded Leopard

Oriental Small-clawed Otter

Masked Palm Civet

Bearded Pig

Leopard Cat

Mouse Deer

Barking Deer

Sambar Deer

Bare or muddy areas in the forest or along roads are worth investigating for animal tracks, as they can indicate the presence of particular types of animals in the area. Ungulates, such as deer and pig, leave behind hoof prints which are the most commonly seen. Carnivores, such as wild cats and civets, have distinct paw and toe prints, whereas otters show webbed paw and toe prints. All the species of wild cat, except for the Flat-headed Cat (*Felis planiceps*), have retractable claws which do not appear in their footprints; however, civet footprints do show clawmarks, as they cannot retract their claws.

Night insects

While nocturnal mammals are most commonly seen by people who actively look for them, insects are far more obliging. In only a few minutes back at your camp or quarters, you will see many different types of insect visiting your lamp. The myriad shapes and forms insects take are amazing; there are probably over 200,000 different kinds, from the smallest beetles to some of the largest beautiful moths imaginable. Sandflies and mosquitoes have probably already made your acquaintance but there are other more interesting and pleasant insects to watch for!

Lyssa mentoetius, a pretty brown and white moth common in lowland forest. *(Photo: C.L. Chan)*

Moths are very important pollinators, visiting mostly night-blooming flowers that are strongly perfumed and provided with a floral tube. Many moths have a highly developed sense of hearing. In some cases, this may be to detect the echo-location signals of insectivorous bats hunting prey. Some moths even respond by imitating bat clicks to confuse the bats, while moths take evasive action and escape.

Interesting beetles are also easily encountered, such as the imposing, shiny-black, Three-horned Rhinoceros Beetle (*Chalcosoma möllenkampi*). This has two forward pointing, horn-like projections on its prothorax and another curving upwards from the head. There are also insects which mimic various parts of plants. The stick and leaf insects (order Phasmida) are herbivores and are well camouflaged to deceive predators.

The disproportionately large mandibles of a male Stag Beetle (*Prosopocoelus occipitalis*) distinguish it from the female. *(Photo: C.L. Chan)*

So, as you switch off your light to go to sleep, reflect on the day's adventures in the forest, and look forward to what the next day might hold, should you continue your exploration of Sabah's lowland rain forest.

The Giant Atlas Moth (*Attacus atlas*), with wings spanning 25 cm, is the largest moth in the world. Transparent "windows" characteristically adorn the intricately patterned wings. *(Photo: C.L. Chan)*

Vicious looking, the Three-horned Rhinoceros Beetle (*Chalcosoma möllenkampi*) has horns probably not for defence but for jousting with other males in competing for females. These beetles feed mainly on pulpy fruits and also young rattan shoots. *(Photo: A.Y.C. Chung)*

A female leaf insect (*Phyllium* sp.). Unlike the male which has fully functional wings, the female has a heavy body and is incapable of flight. When it rests motionless, its camouflage deceives most potential predators. *(Photo: C.L. Chan)*

A mating pair of the spine-covered, nocturnally active stick insect, *Haaniella echinata*, the female of which subsequently lays the largest eggs in the insect world. *(Photo: C.L. Chan)*

Slow and deceptive, stick insects, such as this *Lonchodes haematomus*, often stretch themselves into a twig-like form and fall limply to the ground when threatened. *(Photo: C.L. Chan)*

WHAT YOU SHOULD KNOW ABOUT VISITING RAIN FOREST

Travel Essentials
Although rain can occur at any time of the year, showers are generally brief except during the northeast monsoon (November to March) when heavy rain occurs, making this probably the least exciting time to visit lowland forest (unless rain does not dampen your spirits!). Sudden torrential rain storms can arise in the afternoons, sometimes preceded by strong winds. When in the forest, this is a time of danger from falling trees and branches. Shelter should be carefully chosen until the wind has died down.

Vaccinations
None are necessary for a visit to Sabah's rain forest but it is a good idea to be up-to-date with certain immunisations, such as for Hepatitis A and Tetanus. Malarial prophylactics are advisable. Make sure you commence the course two weeks in advance of your trip and carry on for six weeks after you return home.

Clothing and other items
Comfortable cotton clothing is ideal for Sabah's climate. For a trip into the forest, long trousers and long-sleeved shirts are advised and a sturdy pair of training shoes or boots with good soles is needed. Leather boots may be difficult to keep dry. Other useful items to take with you are a compass (even experienced people can get lost in the forest!), torch, binoculars, leech socks (like puttees), spare plastic bags to store your camera in case of rain, water bottle, high-energy food snacks, and a collapsible umbrella.

Safety
Before setting off, make sure you tell someone where you are going and, while in the forest, stay on the trails.

FURTHER READING

Bennett, E.L. & F. Gombek. 1993. *Proboscis Monkeys of Borneo*. Natural History Publications (Borneo) Sdn. Bhd., Kota Kinabalu & KOKOTAS Berhad, Ranau, Sabah.

Chan, C.L., A. Lamb, P.S. Shim & J.J. Wood. 1994. *Orchids of Borneo, Vol. 1. Introduction and a selection of Species*. The Sabah Society, Kota Kinabalu in association with The Royal Botanic Gardens, Kew, England.

Cubbitt, G. & J. Payne. 1990. *Wild Malaysia*. New Holland with World Wide Fund for Nature, United Kingdom.

Dransfield, J. 1984. *The Rattans of Sabah*. Forestry Department, Sabah.

Dransfield, S. 1992. *Bamboos of Sabah*. Forestry Department, Sabah.

Forestry in Sabah. 1989. Forestry Department, Sabah.

Ghazally, I. 1990. *The Living Heritage of Sabah*. Ministry of Tourism and Environmental Development & Sabah Parks Trustees, Sabah.

Inger, R.F. 1962. *The Systematics and Zoogeography of the Amphibia of Borneo*. Fieldiana 52: 1-402. Reprinted in 1990 by Lun Hing Trading Company, Kota Kinabalu.

Inger, R.F. & P.K. Chin. 1962. *The Fresh-water Fishes of North Borneo*. Fieldiana 45: 1-268. Reprinted and updated 1990 by The Sabah Zoological Society, Kota Kinabalu.

Inger, R.F. & R. Steubing. 1992. *Frogs of Sabah*. Sabah Parks Trustees, Kota Kinabalu.

Kamarudin Mat Salleh. 1991. *Rafflesia - Magnificent Flower of Sabah*. Borneo Publishing Company, Kota Kinabalu.

Meijer, W. & G.H.S. Wood. 1964. *Dipterocarps of Sabah (North Borneo)*. Forestry Department, Sabah.

Payne, J. & M. Andau. 1989. *Orang-Utan, Malaysia's Mascot*. Berita Publishing Sdn. Bhd., Kuala Lumpur.

Payne, J., C. M. Francis & K. Phillipps. 1985 *A Field Guide to the Mammals of Borneo*. The Sabah Society, Kota Kinabalu, with Worldwide Fund for Nature, Kuala Lumpur.

Smythies, B.E. 1960. *The Birds of Borneo*. 3rd ed. 1981, rev. Earl of Cranbrook. The Sabah Society, Kota Kinabalu, with Malayan Nature Society, Kuala Lumpur.

Tan, F.L. 1993. *Checklist of Lizards of Sabah*. Sabah Parks Trustees, Kota Kinabalu, Sabah.

Thapa, R.S. 1981. *Termites of Sabah*. Forestry Department, Sabah.

Vermeulen, J.J. 1990. *Orchids of Borneo, Vol. 2. Bulbophyllum*. Toihaan Publishing Company Sdn. Bhd., Kota Kinabalu & Bentham-Moxon Trust, Royal Botanic Gardens, Kew, England.

Wong, K.M. 1990. *In Brunei Forests: An Introduction to the Plant Life of Brunei Darussalam*. Forestry Department, Ministry of Industry and Primary Resources, Brunei Darussalam.

Yates, S. 1992. *The Nature of Borneo*. Facts On File, New York, U.S.A.

ACKNOWLEDGEMENTS

Many people have assisted in turning my desire to write a book about rain forest into reality and I should first like to thank two people, Dr Clive Marsh, Innoprise Corporation Sdn. Bhd., for inviting me to write the book and Tengku D.Z. Adlin, President of the Sabah Society and Deputy Director of the Sabah Foundation, for his wholehearted support of the project. I especially wish to thank my husband, Joseph Gasis, for his ideas and for suggesting the form the book should take. Several people and institutions have also played an important role while I have been in Sabah and I would like to take this opportunity to thank them. Thank you to Dr D. Newbery, University of Stirling, U.K., who was responsible for sending me to Sabah in the first place, the Royal Botanic Garden, Edinburgh, U.K. and in particular Dr G. Argent who has been a continuous source of encouragement to me in my botanical work, and the Royal Society of London, U.K. who have provided financial assistance during my early studies on rain forest plants. A special thank you goes to Mr Leopold Madani, Encik Berhaman Ahmad, and all of the herbarium staff at the Forest Research Centre, Sepilok, for always making me feel welcome during my many visits over the years. Thanks go to friends who diligently read and made useful comments, suggestions and corrections to the manuscript, Dr M. Heydon, Ms N. Ghaffar, Ms M. Pinard, Dr J. Willott, Ms S. Yorath, Mr R. Rajanathan, Mr A. Lamb, Ms A. Phillipps and Dr C. Marsh.

I would also like to thank everyone who has generously allowed their slides to be published, Mr C.L. Chan, Mr A.Y.C. Chung, Dr M. Heydon, Mr A. Lamb, Mr F. Lanting, Mr W.M. Poon, Mr M. Strange, Mr R.B. Stuebing, Dr B.S. Parris and Dr K.M. Wong. Thanks must also go to Dr J.D. Holloway, Dr R.F. Inger, Mr R.B. Stuebing, Mr C.L. Chan, Dr J. Dransfield, Dr K.M. Wong, and Datuk P.K. Chin for kindly identifying the subjects on many of the slides. I would also like to thank Mr Jamal Hassim and Mr C.L. Chan for the superb line illustrations and Ms Chee Fui Nee and Ms Lucy F.L. Liew for the typing of the manuscript. A very special thank you goes to Chan Chew Lun who has spent much valuable time and effort in the book's production and has managed to remain cheerful and optimistic throughout! My thanks go to Wong Khoon Meng, who was responsible for the time-consuming task of editing the book and preparing the index, as well as helping to write or reshape captions to the photographs. Finally, I would like to thank my family for their support over the years.

INDEX

About The Author

Elaine J.F. Campbell first came to study the forests of Sabah in 1985, as a research assistant on a field project based at the Danum Valley Field Centre, where she fell in love with the rain forest. A botanist who has written for the European Garden Flora and participated in the Flora Of Bhutan, she is now also contributing revisions to the Tree Flora of Sabah and Sarawak, and involved with scientific projects of the British Overseas Development Administration based in Kalimantan. Trained at Edinburgh and Stirling, she now resides in Lahad Datu in eastern Sabah, from where she regularly visits different rain forest areas, sometimes bringing friends and associates on tours of her favourite outdoor "habitat". This is her first book introducing the rain forest, although she has written a number of ecological and botanical papers based on her work in the forests of Sabah.

For discerning visitors to Malaysia who yearn to see wildlife in a primeval Borneo rainforest and to understand the conservation realities of our times, we believe we have the right destination.

Borneo Rainforest Lodge is designed by naturalists, built with local materials and located in a magnificent setting beside the Danum River in Sabah's largest protected lowland forest — the Danum Valley Conservation Area. The Lodge has developed out of the success of the nearby Danum Valley Field Centre, one of the foremost research and environmental education establishments in South East Asia. We hope to demonstrate that appropriate tourism can play an important positive role in rainforest protection.

Photo: C. Marsh

BORNEO RAINFOREST LODGE

Block D, Lot 10, Sadong Jaya Complex
P.O. Box 11622
88817 Kota Kinabalu
Sabah, Malaysia

Tel: 088-243245
Fax: 088-243244 TLX: MA80800 SAFOND

Borneo Rainforest Lodge is owned and managed by Innoprise Corporation Sdn. Bhd., the commercial arm of the Sabah Foundation.

SABAH

Malaysia

BORNEO'S PARADISE

SABAH – MALAYSIA'S NATURAL WONDER. HER RICH FLORA AND FAUNA AWAIT TO BE EXPLORED.

WITH OVER 3 MILLION HECTARES OF GAZETTED FOREST RESERVES SABAH OFFERS THE WORLD COMPLEX AND UNIQUE ECOSYSTEMS WHICH ARE THE OLDEST IN THE WORLD. THROUGH PRUDENT PRESERVATION AND CONSERVATION MEASURES, SABAH'S TROPICAL RAINFORESTS ARE BEING PROTECTED FOR THE FUTURE.

IN SABAH ONE CAN ENJOY WALKS AMONGST GIANT HARDWOOD TREES, SOME HUNDREDS OF YEARS OLD, AND TAKE IN THE SIGHTS AND SOUNDS OF THIS ANCIENT FOREST WHICH TEEMS WITH MILLIONS OF SPECIES OF WILDLIFE.

SABAH TOURISM PROMOTION CORPORATION

Postal Address
Mail Bag 112,
88999 Kota Kinabalu, Sabah,
Malaysia.

Location Address
No. 51, Jalan Gaya,
88000 Kota Kinabalu, Sabah,
Malaysia.

Tel: (088) 218620, 212121,
219310, 219311, 219400
Telex: SABTOP MA 80244
Cable: SABTOP
Fax: (088)-212075

CCAS/STPC/258